Avoid Exploring with Captain Cook!

Fancy a life on the ocean wave?

The Danger Zone

Written by
Mark Bergin

Illustrated by
David Antram

Created and designed by
David Salariya

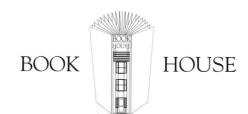

BOOK HOUSE

Contents

Introduction

t's the year 1768. King George III is on the throne and Britain is expanding its horizons and finding new territories. You are sixteen-year-old Isaac Smith, and you hope to find adventure and excitement when you join the Royal Navy. James Cook, a relative of yours is a well-respected ship's commander. Your parents have persuaded him to let you sail with him, and you're all ready to go. There's an expedition to Tahiti, all set to leave harbour. What will you see on the way? What will it be like when you get there? You have heard strange stories of people, lands, and animals on the other side of the world. Will the people be friendly or are they bloodthirsty cannibals? You think it's going to be fun – but how much do you really know about becoming a sailor? Are you sure you want to sail to the other side of the world? The voyage will take three long years – but you don't know this yet. You will have to learn the ropes and get used to your new shipmates. Your life on board an eighteenth-century square-rigged ship will be hard and dangerous – and you'll have to behave yourself, or you'll be flogged! You may learn that you wouldn't want to sail with Captain Cook!

Pressed into Service!

You're lucky that your parents know Captain Cook. They have asked him to take you as midshipman (trainee officer) on his next voyage. For other sailors, things aren't so easy. Normally, Press Gangs recruit men to serve in the lower ranks of the Royal Navy. Squads of sailors go to public houses to round-up men aged between 16 and 35. Drunks are often bundled away for a life at sea before they know what's happening. Troublesome men are knocked on the head – and they wake up on board ship! Magistrates often give tramps, criminals and smugglers who appear in their courts a choice: join the Navy or go to prison!

ISAAC SMITH age 16

LUCKY BREAK. Captain James Cook will take you on board his ship.

Hmmm ... Have you ever been to sea before, young man?

Cook's Mission

 aptain Cook's mission is to observe the transit of Venus across the face of the Sun above the skies of Tahiti. There was a transit in 1761. Astronomers took over 120 measurements from all over the world of that transit, but their results were too varied to be useful. The next transit will be on 3rd June, 1769 – and then not again for another 105 years! So the mission is urgent. After this is done, Captain Cook also has some secret orders. For many years there has been talk of a great southern continent, Terra Australis Incognita. Cook will look for, and then chart this land.

The route of The Endeavour:

The *Endeavour* sailed to Tahiti via South America.

TELESCOPE. On-board astronomer Charles Green will use this to observe the transit.

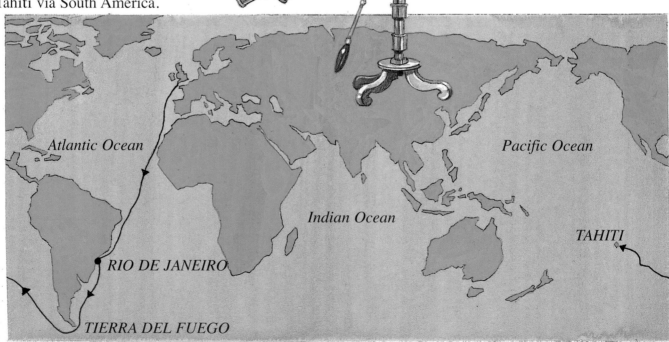

Atlantic Ocean

Pacific Ocean

Indian Ocean

RIO DE JANEIRO

TAHITI

TIERRA DEL FUEGO

Cast Off!

Your ship is an ex-Whitby collier (coal-carrier), the *Earl of Pembroke*, bought by the Navy for £2,800 and renamed the *Endeavour*. It has been refitted, with extra cabins for the officers and scientists. Captain Cook likes colliers because they have a shallow draught (this means they don't sit too deeply in the water). The Admiralty describes the *Endeavour* as "fit to stow provisions and stores." It is 32 m long, 10 m across at its widest, and about 4 m deep.

MEET YOUR MATES. Make friends with your shipmates, however frightening they look! Remember, you'll be spending the next three years with them.

We'll show you the ropes.

Handy hint

Get to know nautical names for parts of the ship. You'll need to know what everyone's talking about!

THE *ENDEAVOUR*. There are three masts: the fore, main and mizzen. The main is about 37 m high. These masts are supported by ropes called stays and shrouds. Ratlines, fixed to the shrouds, form ladders.

11

Keeping a Tight Ship

Discipline and punishment on board ship is hard. Punishment is often flogging – being whipped with a special whip called a 'cat-o-nine-tails.' The phrase 'over a barrel' means being tied over a gun barrel to be flogged. Captain Cook knows that if he doesn't give enough lashes, the crew won't respect him, but if he gives too many, they might mutiny! On 16th September 1768, Henry Stephens gets 12 lashes for refusing to eat his allowance of fresh beef – sailors are used to salted meat. But Captain Cook is a reasonable man for his time and, in the three years of the voyage, he only punishes 21 of the crew. The normal number of lashes is 12, though two men who desert get 24.

Good discipline

Good discipline means that the ship is well ordered. Men are punished if they fail to do their duty and put the ship and crew in danger. Some of the worst offences are falling asleep on duty, refusing to follow orders, or 'unclean behaviour,' that is relieving yourself on the ship rather than using the toilet facilities.

They rub salt into the wounds too.

Jobs on board The Endeavour:

SAIL-MAKER. He is a vital member of the crew. He mends torn and worn sails, and sometimes makes new ones.

PAINTING. Paint protects the wood and makes a good impression in port. It also keeps the crew out of mischief!

CAULKING. The crew hammer greased hemp rope fibres into the plank seams of the decks to keep the water out.

"SWAB THE DECKS!" This means cleaning the decks. It is done every morning by swabbers.

Watch Out – Officers!

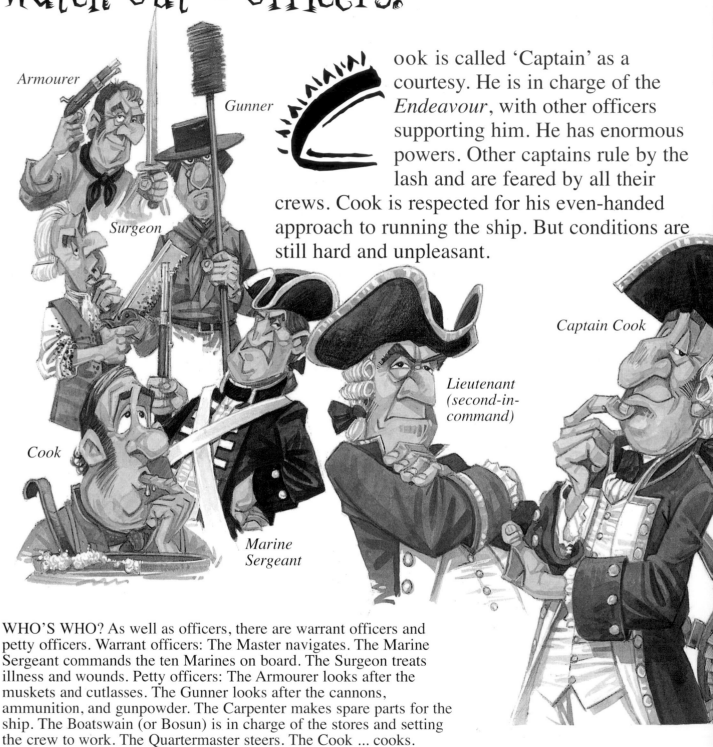

Cook is called 'Captain' as a courtesy. He is in charge of the *Endeavour*, with other officers supporting him. He has enormous powers. Other captains rule by the lash and are feared by all their crews. Cook is respected for his even-handed approach to running the ship. But conditions are still hard and unpleasant.

Armourer

Gunner

Surgeon

Cook

Marine Sergeant

Lieutenant (second-in-command)

Captain Cook

WHO'S WHO? As well as officers, there are warrant officers and petty officers. Warrant officers: The Master navigates. The Marine Sergeant commands the ten Marines on board. The Surgeon treats illness and wounds. Petty officers: The Armourer looks after the muskets and cutlasses. The Gunner looks after the cannons, ammunition, and gunpowder. The Carpenter makes spare parts for the ship. The Boatswain (or Bosun) is in charge of the stores and setting the crew to work. The Quartermaster steers. The Cook ... cooks.

14

Disagreements and fights sometimes break out, and it is up to the officers on board and, finally, the Captain to make sure the ship runs smoothly and everything is ship-shape! As a Midshipman, if you want to become a full officer, you will need to take your lieutenant's examination in six years.

Handy hint

Follow your orders well and quickly, and you'll get on fine with Captain Cook!

Joseph Banks (Botanist)

Quartermaster

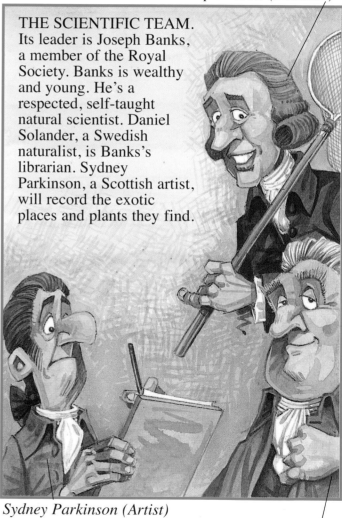

THE SCIENTIFIC TEAM. Its leader is Joseph Banks, a member of the Royal Society. Banks is wealthy and young. He's a respected, self-taught natural scientist. Daniel Solander, a Swedish naturalist, is Banks's librarian. Sydney Parkinson, a Scottish artist, will record the exotic places and plants they find.

Sydney Parkinson (Artist)

Daniel Solander (Naturalist)

Accidents Will Happen...

Watch out while you are on board ship! Accidents can happen anytime on long sea voyages on a square-rigger. The ship is complicated to sail, and there's always the danger that a sailor can fall from the rigging or overboard, or the ship could hit an uncharted reef, and everyone could be drowned. Knowing your ropes is crucial – not knowing them can kill you! When the *Endeavour* reaches Funchal, the capital of Madeira, the quartermaster, Alexander Weir, gets tangled up in the anchor's guide rope. He is dragged to the bottom of the sea and drowned.

TOO MUCH RUM. John Reading, age 24, dies from alcohol poisoning.

SUICIDE. Marine Private William Greenslade commits suicide by jumping overboard after being accused of theft.

DROWNED. Peter Flowers, age 18, drowns at Rio de Janeiro. He has served with Captain Cook for five years.

Rations: Food and Drink

The *Endeavour* is packed with food for 90 men for 12 months. This includes 4,000 pieces of salt beef, 6,000 pieces of salt pork and 360 kg of suet (fat). There is also wheat, oatmeal, and bread, 545 litres of oil and 680 kg of sugar. And, for the thirsty crew, there are 5,455 litres of beer and 7,270 litres of spirits! There's even tobacco for the men to buy. Officers enjoy fresh meat from live animals, which also provide fresh eggs and milk. But the sailors like what they are used to – they prefer salted meat to fresh!

Dinner is served!

Not more fresh meat!

18

I need the limes to help my teeth stay healthy!

Handy hint

It's best to eat the ship's biscuits in the dark, so you can't see the weevils!

SAUERKRAUT. This pickled cabbage contains vitamins that help prevent a disease called scurvy, which makes your teeth fall out. There is 3565 kg of it on board. But the men will only eat it after they see the officers eating it. Limes and syrup of lemons can also help to prevent outbreaks of scurvy.

19

Landfall!

After stopping at the Atlantic island of Madeira, you cross the Equator, and pick up supplies at Rio de Janeiro, in Brazil. Finally you reach Cape Horn. Joseph Banks and his team collect specimens at Tierra del Fuego, and Cook makes surveys of sheltered places to anchor.

Soon, you are clear of stormy Cape Horn. The *Endeavour* sails northwest to the newly-discovered island of Tahiti in the Pacific. You reach it on 13th April 1769 – in time to observe the transit of Venus in June.

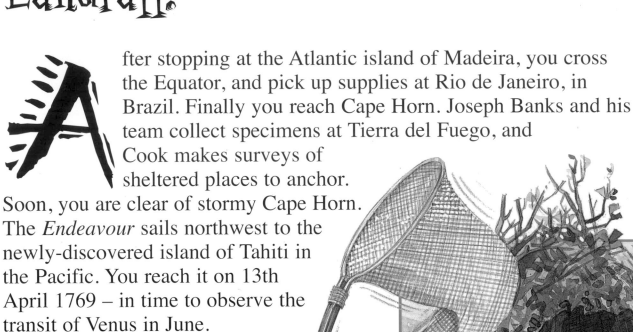

JOSEPH BANKS. He collects specimens from wherever he can, and takes them back to the ship to study.

TIERRA DEL FUEGO. The people here live in huts of woven tree-trunks. Captain Cook writes, "They are neither proof against wind, hail, rain or snow… these people must be a hardy race."

Handy hint

Never look at the sun through a telescope. You will burn your eyes and go BLIND!!

I hope the sky's not cloudy!

THE PEOPLE OF TAHITI. These friendly people don't understand private property. They'll take anything that's left lying around! (below)

COOK'S OBSERVATIONS Captain Cook recorded his observations of the transit (as shown right).

Tattoos and Canoes

aptain Cook's orders are to find Terra Australis, so you sail west from Tahiti in July 1769. On 6th October 1769, Nicholas Young, age 12, sights land – it's New Zealand. The people here are very different from the easy-going Tahitians. They are Maoris – tough, brave warriors who attack the ship. The crew use firearms against them, killing several of them at a place Cook names Poverty Bay. In the coming months, Captain Cook charts the entire North and South Islands of New Zealand.

TATTOOS. Maori warriors with elaborately tattooed faces come out in their canoes to greet you. Tattooing is new and strange to you. After they discover how it is done, it becomes popular with the British sailors.

Great Barrier of Grief!

After charting New Zealand, you sail north-west to find Terra Australis. On 18th January, Lieutenant Hicks sights land. On 28th April, you drop anchor. Joseph Banks and his team collect a great number of new plants. There are so many that Cook names the place Botany Bay. Then you sail north again. Captain Cook is the first to chart the entire east coast of Australia.

NO THANKS. The Australian aborigines are not interested in trading or gifts.

CRASH! At the Great Barrier Reef, the ship strikes coral! A bandage made from a sail filled with wool and oakum is dragged over the hole. Water pressure keeps it in place.

NEW PLANTS AND ANIMALS. When Joseph Banks and Daniel Solander land in Botany Bay, they collect many species of plants and animals, all unknown in Europe.

Handy hint

Be the first to land at Botany Bay. You'll go down in history books!

SOUNDINGS. The crew take soundings to get the ship through the reefs. On the shore, they spend six weeks on repairs.

SAVE WEIGHT. To help refloat the ship, anchors, guns, cannon balls, iron pots and spare timbers are thrown overboard.

STUCK ON THE REEF. You and the crew work the pumps and plug the hole. After 24 hours, you manage to refloat the ship. You use longboats to tow it off the reef.

Come on! We've been stuck on this reef for 12 hours!

Disease, done for, and death!

Leaving Australia, Cook puts in to the island of Savu for fresh supplies. The crew are in good health. Then you sail to Batavia (now called Jakarta), a Dutch settlement. You dock there in October 1770. Soon, men start to get sick with malaria. The disease takes hold. The first to die is the surgeon, William Monkhouse, on 5th November. Tents are set up ashore, where the sick can be better looked after. As you start for Cape Town, South Africa, 40 men are on the sick list. In 1771, between January and February, many of your shipmates die. Eleven are buried at sea in one week! In all, a third of the crew die of malaria and dysentery, which is also called the 'bloody flux.'

BURIAL AT SEA. When a sailor dies, the sail-maker sews him into his hammock. A stitch is put through his nose to check he is dead. Cannon shot inside the canvas makes sure the body sinks.

WILLIAM MONKHOUSE. William Monkhouse is the surgeon until he dies. If a sick bay is needed at sea, a small area is canvassed off.

Land Ahoy!

On 13th July, 1771, Nicholas Young sights Land's End, in Cornwall. You and your shipmates are excited to see the coast of England after three years at sea. The voyage has been a great success, apart from the crew losses. Cook has fulfilled the Admiralty's and the Royal Society's orders – the transit of Venus has been observed. The entire coastline of New Zealand is charted, and the coast of eastern Australia is mapped too.

MADEIRA

Atlantic Ocean

RIO DE JANEIRO

CAPE TOWN

TIERRA DEL FUEGO

THE ROUTE. This map shows the *Endeavour*'s route on the voyage between 1768-1771. This will become the blueprint for Captain Cook's future voyages in the South Seas.

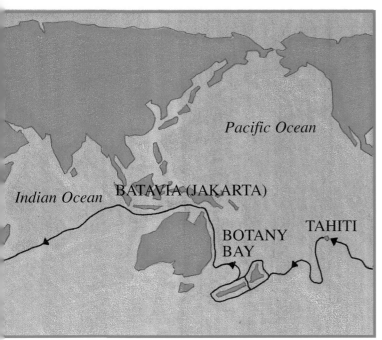

Pacific Ocean

Indian Ocean

BATAVIA (JAKARTA)

BOTANY BAY

TAHITI

Handy hint

Bring something from your travels as a gift for your parents!

HOME AGAIN! Your parents hardly recognise you. You join Captain Cook as master mate on the second voyage, on the *Resolution*. In 1787, you become a captain. In 1807, you're made a Rear Admiral!

NEW LAND TO RULE. The government can now see new places for Britain to rule. Captain Cook is soon sent on a second expedition in two larger ships: *Resolution* and *Adventure*, 1772-75.

Welcome home my boy! What have you brought me?

Glossary

Admiralty The government department responsible for the Royal Navy.

Astronomer A scientist who studies the stars and other heavenly bodies.

Brimstone The old word for sulphur.

Boatswain/Bosun The officer in charge of the sails and rigging. His duties include rousing the men for their duty.

Botanists Scientists who study plant life.

Chart To make a map of coastlines in detail so ships can navigate. It can also mean the map itself.

Cutlass A short sword with a slightly curved blade used by sailors.

Dysentery An infectious disease that causes very bad diarrhoea.

Equator An imaginary line making a circle around Earth, halfway between the North and South Poles.

Fumigate To use smoke to kill germs and parasites such as lice.

Grog A seaman's daily allowance of rum.

Malaria A fever caused by a tiny parasite, carried and spread by mosquitoes.

Oakum Loose fibres made by picking old rope into pieces.

Ratline A short rope fastened across two shrouds to form a ladder on a ship.

Rigging The ropes, sails, and stays of a ship.

Scurvy A serious disease that many sailors used to suffer from, caused by a lack of Vitamin C. This was because they did not often get to eat fresh fruit and vegetables.

Shrouds A set of ropes forming the rigging for the masts.

Square-rigger A sailing ship with the sail rig set at right angles to the mast and keel.

Transit The route of a star or planet as seen from Earth.

Index